for Gaynell Begley

The people returned here briefly and held orange rinds wrapped in cloth over their mouths as they gathered the dead, listing their names . . . .

—Carolyn Forché

winner of the 2007 Kore Press First Book Award

selected by *Sonia Sanchez*

Benjamin's Spectacles

Spring Ulmer

KORE PRESS   TUCSON

Di –

So you, who know my slant
who can intuit the need
to stay true to something
inside...
I wish you so much luck
with medicine –
& finding the internal
meaning of
things ♥ Spring

Kore Press, Inc.
Tucson, Arizona USA
WWW.KOREPRESS.ORG

ISBN13 978-1-888553-22-2
ISBN10 1-888553-22-7

 Designed by Lisa Bowden

PREVIOUS FIRST BOOK AWARD WINNERS: Jennifer Barber for *Rigging the Wind*, selected by Jane Miller; Deborah Fries for *Various Modes of Departure*, selected by Carolyn Forché; Elline Lipkin for *The Errant Thread*, selected by Eavan Boland; Sandra Lim for *Loveliest Grotesque*, selected by Marilyn Chin.

We express our deep gratitude to those who helped make this Kore Press First Book Award possible: The Tucson Pima Arts Council, The Arizona Commission on the Arts, through appropriations from the Arizona State Legislature and the National Endowment for the Arts, the manuscript readers, the judge, and all the writers who submitted their work.

contents

Benjamin's Spectacles

Intersection of the Belly and the Mirror

A
half-darkened room (39) fat, tired sheep (52) We will live in them like melons (56)

B
the whores as a battle memorial (63) velvet cushions on clouds (64) "Riverbank in Spring" (68) a body that never knows its full nakedness (68)

C
stone quarries all interconnected (89) a stone slab in which there is a small hole (90)

D
the weather is like in war (101)

E
Entwicklung der Photographie (131) artist unknown (134)

F
winding iron staircases (163) balloon's-eye view (165)

G
woman in white (172) An image of the everyday (174) frothy life (176) a sandwich-man seen from the back (179) not only faces but living flesh (197)

H
sets of teeth (203) Brittle, too, are Mirrors (204) (birds, ants) (211)

I
face on the totem pole (212) "What is the height of your embarrassment?" (217) The shell bears the impression of its occupant (220) hotel rooms; for the dead (221) The belly overspreads (225)

From: Benjamin, Walter. *The Arcades Project.* Trans. by Howard Eiland and Kevin McLaughlin; prepared on the basis of the German volume edited by Rolf Tiedemann. Cambridge, Mass.; London : Belknap Press, 1999.

Walter Benjamin at the Epic Theater

There is a mixing of parts, scenes, sounds. Let me list them in no order of appearance.

There is Walter Benjamin.

There is Bertolt Brecht's fanatical study of a Chinese method of acting in which the actor plays himself playing the part, marveling at himself as another. But, when Brecht's wife plays Mother Courage (the sinewy troubadour with a malleable face who clangs coffee pots together), she grows angry at herself for playing the role of a stupid woman.

This is the power of an actress, lonely on stage (her role always before having been played by a man who sang through his nose), the smell of wild garlic on her.

A nameless, manly old woman haunts the terraced hillside around the theater. She supports herself by smuggling Marlboros across the border. In the stories she tells, the women characters are all six feet tall. These stories are dateless, like the spot she points to, remembering the coal town. There is nothing there but grass, yet I look twice—

Theater is as much the strangeness of the storyteller, as it is falling into the storyteller's snare. (*Do you want some oatmeal with raisons?* the old woman calls from her terraced path, wrinkling her nose at me. She knows I don't like raisons.) Moreover, it is about what a spectator promises.

Now that I am caught in the old woman's snare, I will have to visit her from time to time. The hill she lives on will be mined, then bulldozed into four lanes. She will buy a washer-dryer. The city will eventually steal the old woman's garden, but she'll keep planting it. (In the city, people are handcuffing themselves to garden fences at this moment.)

The performers' discarded—there is no show, Benjamin is just wandering around the theater—long cuffs and gnome-like shoes (pointed and upturned) lie crumpled on the floor. Benjamin, completely out of character, lifts up a pair of pantaloons and sticks in one foot and then the other, pulling them on. They fit him tightly and the jacket makes it hard for him to wave his arms. He's conscious of belonging, however halfheartedly, to History (or at least its End), as he bangs on a drum and sings a childish melody.

I stand in the wing and take notes.

Allegory 1

My father sits in a brown armchair,
iron poker by the fire. I am dressed
like Walter Benjamin, my breasts
in shadow. I stoke the fire.
From shadow to shadow,
unattainable self to unattainable self.
My father's hands move a dowel.
Checkmate, he says. I poke the fire.
I have been his son. *Look at those arms.*
He admires my muscles. The nudity of words.
Don't choke the fire. My mother is outside smoking.
I am my mother's daughter. Impotency in the face
of king and queen towers, smoking,
on fire. Beckett said he had no feelings.
My mother looks like Beckett with her bird hair
beyond the window. My father and I soak in the fire.
Shadows beckon. Nothing is its own pure self.
I cannot move. My father wins, but not
without my hunchbacked help.

The Distance Between Self and Other

Benjamin, like Brecht,
believed the reader

should become author,
                    I inherited my mother's want
and so he ceased cultivating
                    to perfect the earth.
his notebooks and disappeared
into his texts.
                    After a time I became completely
                    infected by earth—
Meanwhile, Adorno argued
authors must mediate
                    controlled, meek,
                    part of my mother's garden—
their texts,
                    something to eat.
and so he continued to
                    She was sustained by
                    rooting, planting, and protecting
translate what Benjamin
                    earthworms. I ate nothing
thought inherently untranslatable.
                    but leaves, stems—
                    spring greens.

Geographyless

Behind razor wire, refugees
sew their mouths shut.

The TV's on mute.

An old woman is saving cantaloupe seeds,
though yesterday she told me she wouldn't
grow another garden.

Do you keep them wet or dry them? I ask.

Dry them.

Seeded nothingness.

The old woman doesn't believe I'm a girl.
I don't carry a purse, wear a bra, bleed.

I tell her I'm Walter Benjamin.

Who's that? she asks.

Do I say he believed if art could starve
its aura, balloon its skeleton for the world to view,
there might be hope against the fury of today?

One of those refugees, I answer.

She looks confused.

But you're not!

On Benjamin's Aunt's Table

A mine entombed in glass

I was always attracted to girlish

in which little men push

boys, skinny ones, and to dark

tiny wheelbarrows, toil with

roads (oiled to keep dust down);

pickaxes, and shine lanterns
into the shafts in which

an old town named Hot Spot;
coalfield tipples' long shadows;

transport baskets are always
moving up and down.

the raping and pillaging hidden
behind leaves the size of windshields.

Such digging in which nothing
is ever brought to the surface,

'The wished for wound,'
my father called my attraction
to destruction.

Benjamin will later theorize,

I wanted to arrest time, stop

is what actually breaks through,

the action with my camera,
so as to visit the imprisoned,

freeing history from itself.

dressed in pink, their eyes on me.

On Benjamin's Girlfriend's Table

Benjamin at 19, a delirious shepherd grown into the shape of a long scythe.

Benjamin—the last wreckage—dancing, self-consciously, under the stairs.

The *Vicente* in Caravaggio's painting.

Brown curls.

A woman kisses him in public. The policeman's light finds her.

Later, Benjamin uncloaks, climbs a tree, then lies out on the grass. The woman listens to the wind beat her back.

What happens has nothing to do with the size of the leaves, nothing to do with the moon hanging, oppressively, in the middle of a one-way street.

What happens is that the door has a footprint on it. Benjamin wears a red shirt.

Desire bottled up near the old barn with the thrown away flowers.

Afraid she is pregnant, the woman would like to have Benjamin's baby, but Benjamin can barely hold her.

The mountain inside her becomes a mine. She loses weight, feels like his belt-loop.

He reads a poem at her white-leaved table, voice cracking.

She picks tiger lilies and puts them in a trash bag. He puts the trash bag in the trunk of his red car.

The mountains, she thinks, will leave with him. She does not want to let go.

She accuses him of having more power. He asks, wide-eyed, *How do I have more power?*

Her neighbor children say he looks like a girl and she, a boy.

They look like each other. Scarves, garlic odor, moon eyes . . .

I stumble in on her, alone, starved up there on the hill where she pretends to write, Benjamin's blue fingerprints on her table.

Post-Strange Fruit

I

One evening a man
with a machete
chopped
an arm-
pit of grass
between cracks
in the side-
walk just east
of Western.

I can still
hear the clip-
ping sound
of that grey,
mean, country
louse attacking
every blade
of grass.

II

Those who live
through genocide
survive, believing
they have already
died.

III

Grape-
fruits
hang
plenti-
fully
on my
dwarf
tree.

The yellow suns
drop to the ground,
holes drilled in
their sour
skin by insects,
worms.

IV

Glazed
pot-
bellied
jugs
sit like
resigned,
old men in
the corner
of the court-
yard, sweat-
ing. Pigeons
waddle.

V

Near-
sighted,
I try to
memorize
what blurs:
Mountains just blobs;
people unrecognizable
in a mass grave;
tortured bodies
wrapped
in plastic,
iced so
they don't
bruise.

Fairy Tales

I

My father tells me Clean Fill Wanted is a wanted man.

> *Benjamin's letters look like gnats. He dips his pen in ink, blots, crosses*
> *out, attempts one-hundred lines per page. Bent over, he looks like his*
> *mother in the snowy window engrossed in her needlework.*

Mr. Squiggly's going to the post office, my father says when it snows sideways, flakes
scurrying across the road, wind erasing our tracks.

I sit on his tool box, so I can see out the truck window, laughing whenever we hit a
bump and my head hits the cab's ceiling. I love being light, the snow falling outside.

> *Despite his embroidered, upright script, Benjamin fumbles the flowery china,*
> *the blue onion box so weighty. 'Greetings to Mr. Clumbsy!' his mother says*
> *when he drops his knife. He runs from the table back to his squid pen, the*
> *liquid blue black stain trailing across the paper's cream.*

II

In my room, I feed my ventriloquist, assuming if his jaw opens, he must chew. He
seems so empty, hair waxed, eyes too wide, body rail thin, animated, eager.

I want to fill him. Orange juice dribbles out his neck, down his back and stings my
nail-bitten fingers. My mother was punished for biting—

> *Years later Benjamin will marry. His wife's name will sound like 'door.' Benjamin*
> *will run from her to Brecht's protégé. Thereafter, Brecht will spot Benjamin*
> *crying, suitcase on his knee.*

My grandmother poisoned my mother, applying layers of chemical polish to her nails
until the blood red apple in Snow White shimmered on the end of each one of my
mother's unlucky fingers.

> *Pressing down on the gold nib of his fountain pen, using his suitcase as a table,*
> *Benjamin will trace the topography of his journey.*

Benjamin's mother, finger-thimbled, will receive a postcard of peaked lines.

III

There's a stage-coach robber and a slave ship driver in my past. To an escaping slave the moon is an omen—a white jellyfish, floating, phosphorescent. I pick at the glow-in-the-dark stickers on my wall.

> *'All intimacies are sacrificed to the illuminations of detail ... one will have to get used to being looked at,' Benjamin will write, his mother's Braille-like touch influencing his exaggerated world-view, his need to be famous, beheld, seen.*

I take down the moon and all the stars, too.

IV

On the way to the post office, I nibble sickle moons off each finger.

> *Benjamin will woo a woman to assist him in procuring the children's books his wife claims are hers. Divorce, worse than the throws of his marriage's darkest rows.*

When we get there, I hop out of the truck and run up the steps, through the swinging glass doors. With my little key I empty the gold box and unstuff the letters impatiently.

> *He'll dream of horned fish and monsters advancing, cabbageheads plummeting from towering stalks, vertigo claiming their violet weight—*

I want to open them not for what they may say, but because their white envelopes are too bright.

V

Under kerosene lamp light, my invisible (lemon juice) ink can be read. I'm trying it out, writing secret missives, when my mother calls me.

> *Benjamin will be a father and in no time, his son, Stephan, will act up.*

I hurry to the clothesline by my demented apple tree that grows sideways for a cloth to cover my mother who is lying naked in the sun.

Stephan will blame him for failing to be a father.

She's heard a car. I cover her. Minutes later, the armless man arrives.

When the soldiers come, Stephan will already have escaped with his mother. And Benjamin?

It was the armless man's farm I biked home from, a kitten down my shirt, too small to be taken from its mother. Its stomach swelled. I taught it to pee by rubbing its belly with a wet cloth. It slept with me. Still, I wasn't mother enough.

The man has come to collect it.

The Typewriter

To write his way home, pounding the keys of his Olympia, Benjamin (who normally employs someone else do his typing) must break the glass voice of his childhood into fragments he shakes like dice. Each ding of the carriage's end returns him to the city he can never again love with the same innocence he had when he was one with the creatures of the carousel, dizzy with carnival candies and accordion happiness, his mother the colorful pole around which his beautiful horse with its hard, bumpy mane, revolved. The dolls he played with are locked up, naked and grim, in his grandfather's trunk. He pictures their heavy, glass eyes open in the dark, as he pecks out words, hating the Olympia through which he hears the throws of death near his door. Now his grandfather's clock (it, too, in the trunk) strikes arrhythmically in a final mechanical effort to speak. Benjamin stands. His shadow (looking for all the world like a one-armed charioteer) falls on his manuscript and crawls up the wall of his beloved library, as he grabs the last sheet, roller offering up its skin with a rattlesnake purr, and wraps a bottle of morphine tablets (grey and round) in his own words, packing for the ominous journey he must make, smuggling himself over mountains, a quaking aspen *(un álamo temblón)*, his heart monstrously out of tune.

Double Exposure

                           Benjamin withered. The weather was mild.

                           'Peasant weather,' he thought, falling

Benjamin drank from a puddle of infected forestwater,

but made it to the border, despite his ailing heart,

                           asleep under an olive. He dreamed

only to be turned back to the mountain path

soldiers were already swarming.

                           he could jar language back to life.

He passed the manuscript in his suitcase off

                           No longer be able to make meaning,

and, thinking it safe, popped the round, grey tablets.

                           such language would ground people.

His suicide saved lives,

as border guards took pity on his party,

                           He saw them from far off, collecting olives,

                           ripened seeds.

but what he lived for was lost.

It is cold now. Frost in these mountains.

                           Then he glimpsed his angel, sweating,

Today a suitcase exploded, killing five, including a farmer

                           weak, unable to speak.

in a truck full of cabbages.

                           Benjamin was in a city, offering up

                           the angel's image to save himself, when

Erase the traces! was Brecht's advice.

The cabbages vanished.

                           he awoke, his suit dirty, crumpled,

                           a root driving itself into the small of his back.

'Riverbank in Spring'

Angels entertain war guests with water polo, their brittle arms barely able to hold the melon-shaped ball.

  The melancholy sandwiches the angels back to back.

                    Wings knock.

                         When the
water boils, one angel jumps out, naked, screaming.

                    (She is later accused of over-identifying
with history.)

         The other angel swims past.

                    A photo is snapped of the screaming angel (who
cannot know her full nakedness, for her spectacles have melted).

                         The other angel swims
through the gagging milfoil to shore and eats with her back to everyone, fat and tired in the half-dark.

       When she's done, she shakes off the crumbs, and drapes a boa (made of eyelash
yarn) around her neck, envisioning a room full of mirrors in which she is the master.

                              There are
cabbageworms in the street, near where the first angel's picture appears, whorelike, on a
battle memorial—artist unknown.

              How does one photograph an angel?

                         An angel isn't material,
an angel inhabits—

                    Someone has stuffed a cigarette butt into a small hole in the memorial's
stone slab.

           In the nearby graveyard is a winding, iron staircase to a velvet-cushioned, balloon's
eye view.

       At the top of the stairs sits the second angel with a cell phone.

                         It is her job to
measure the height of angelic embarrassment (in other words, she clandestinely films anything
too human).

         The other angel lugs her black box underground. With no fry pan, magnesium
powder, or revolver, her glass plates pick up nothing but dust, as the camera's curtain falls,
uncomfortably, over her wet wing.

Intersection of the Body and Interment

J

Melancholia I (238) from a piece of wood (259) knife wound in the chest (280) old yellow ivory skull (282) your *pearling* of the detail (296) One tires of living in the country (342) so-called fatherland (359) swamp-flower (359) the dead man (376) the dead woman (376) hollow and fleshless (376)

K

gasworks (389) hangman (393) war, like a fever (397) Good nights … turn so effectively the soil and break through the surface stone of our body (403) We must dig down (404) a visit to the dead city—excavation is necessary (404) Life the skin, dissect: here begin the machines (404)

L

shudder (405) puffing, wheezing (405) street becomes room and the room becomes street (406) horsemen, and horsewomen (432) the tall grass (444) "The Lost Letter" (450)

N

bombers remind us (486)

From Benjamin's *The Arcades Project.*

B's Lost Letter to A

I

Only when you are stone,

and red in a field, can you
really absorb all the fieldnesses.

And look at them, my father
explains, *the snail-like fossils*

are really animals that fell over
when they died.

II

A woman holds her dead son,
a fourteen-year old killed in protest.

Before Antigone was hung, she said,
Behold me, what I suffer because

I have upheld that which is high.

III

The tightrope walker says,
He's mean because he loves you

and doesn't know any other way
to show you, like kicking a dog.

Come to me, broken, come—

even after a year of loving
the woman with the bomb
under her sweater.

My body trills like a cricket.

IV

You said, *I am not a patriot or anything.*
Territory the beginning of war—

I searched for an ethics,
a way to love you that was true

beyond all else. And so I let go.

My own liberation comes
from being able to care

without caring.

It is not what I would look for
in the long term.

Yet, the hideous truth is, it is—

V

Something hurts. Not the nights,
not the lies, not even the fallen.

Something in me, like a dirt road

with grass growing up the middle.

VI

I find the photograph
that has been haunting me

of a man and his son
in homemade bird costumes.

They flap, frozen in mid-stroke,

like the prisoner in his

peaked hood and cloak.

VII

A man is tortured.

He knows he will lose his wife,
his children, and strangely

this gives him the calm

to withstand the electric shocks

and not being allowed to go
to the bathroom.

VIII

Pressured body
melting into stone—

a lion's, only to be
met by sword.

We collapse
to uphold.

IX

There
have been
wars between
hyenas and lions,
gold miners and gorillas—

X

The city is a pack of snarling dogs.

And then there is Reggie.
Reggie is just old.

Mitch, Reggie's owner is waiting
on Reggie to come out of the basement.

If Mitch tries to force Reggie out
and he resists, he'll loose all his energy.

But if he makes it out on his own,
Mitch can take him to the vet.

When I saw Reggie last night,
his paws were dirt-

covered and he was lying
with his head on the earth.

The scene reminded me of Antigone
who wouldn't leave her brother unburied.

The king's orders were for her brother's body
to be left to the wild beasts and birds.

Sentenced to starve to death in a cave
for defying the state, upholding her own truth,

Antigone decided to dig her own grave.

The End of Our Correspondence

B choking on figs. Fresh, ripe, loaded in his mouth, pockets. The fate of his letter to A.

B skinny, walking up an alley way. What happened to the love story?

What happened destroyed so much.

B wanted to see where A would take him. He didn't expect the proud refusal A gave.

I am so famished, I make-believe I'm a fruit.

I touch B's letter to A with my blue-brown skin. Just the edge of it—

Its creamy fold punctures my swollen side. My red insides open.

B's hand reaches into his pocket. He withdraws me and the soiled letter to A. He rips the letter up—

Brings me to his mouth.

This warm sensation, his sucking my insides out, my skin puckered into the shape of deflated bellows—

This, the point at which my fantasy can no longer support itself.

Letters to the Dead

Fresh figs on the counter—
Fellini's 8½—
What happens after betrayal?
I don't want to hold a man's hand—
The hunger it spruces—
That flying green—
A beetle shell—
A wish not to be windexed—
These excommunications—
Thimblefuls of relation—
Inner conversation—
Hopkins' letters to the dead—
Heart-shaped leaves outside my kitchen window tremble—
How it disturbs me—
Knocking food off my fork—
Like a hair shirt—
A man withholding love—
Is this all he can give—
Am I ungrateful?
Gesammelte Briefe, Passagen-Werk, Berliner Chronik, Illuminationen—
The order of books on my table—
Smell of old pages—
The hunger-striker undoes his stitched lips—
Poetry unhanging itself—

The Quiet Spectator

I watch the man with the thick black rubber gloves unfurl a hose from the back of a truck.

A horrible thought: What happens when B is separated from the production of his labor?

Without B's library I lose sight of him among the vines crawling over the ruins.

Of course I can still see the old woman.

About the shirts she wears: One is buttoned up and another she ties around her neck to protect herself from the sun she used to love to bathe in.

The stain on my shirt, woodpecker red.

Clouds skirt the mountains.

The man with gloves has measured and is now filling the underground gas well.

I don't throw bombs, I make films, F says. As if he didn't kill his lovers by not loving them enough.

Each man kills the thing he loves, F's refrain. So Wildean, so wild.

The old woman feels safest in the country. In the city people are blowing themselves up, she says.

Now the dry grass is still.

The wooden enclosure patterned with leaf shadow, the thinnest of leaves cast shadows.

The tree-line grey above the lone, gas-filling figure.

I count the silence. I count it because it was never there before. I could never just look out—

What is peacetime, but the knowledge it won't last?

My tears have dried.

A V of geese. My body banded. I wear a barbed wire tattoo.

Crawdads bury themselves.

Teeth gape from bodies death has left half-way preserved.

Holes cut in black plastic for each plant.

I walk on eggshells; I walk so tenderly my feet cry.

I have walked into the pit of water again.

The sadness of green never ends, meanders into mouths of caves until all is stream.

How things fall into rubble, terror, collapse.

Mines take off hands.

How to withstand life? To continue. The wish to continue. Isn't this it?

Gas drips down into storage tanks beneath the macadam.

I am so tired. I wish to die in the field of the fossils. I wish to pick up my remains and head over to the trashcan.

The voice in my head says, *No, that's not something you can do.*

The ugly voice. And the beautiful woman who wants a child.

I am wounded. I am wounded undoubtedly. This wound is not from capture—it is from the game the cat plays after.

I am the one with short hair, the nurse who becomes the patient. I am the one who is tricked, controlled, who returns to torture—

The light is soft.

One man is missing. The woman with his child inside her offers herself in his place.

I will fight you like a woman, she says. *You in those towers, I will be back.*

Twelve men, breathless, lie trapped inside me. Wake up, dusty miners! Wake up to breakfast at midnight!

I am hungry and they feed me. We eat hummus and dates. Pits become heads; the dark flesh, bags.

A sign outside the gate: *America is a friend*—

Lines of thin, thin boys cross the desert. They eat twigs, dirt.

The body washer, under a watermelon moon, rubs metal out of skin.

The lion attacks the bull without cause. Pouring blood falls in patterns.

The gloved man reaches into the earth, transfers the hose to another hole.

A can of Red Bull glitters (sticky, sweet juice dripping from its tab), half-crushed in the gutter alongside a yucca seed pod.

Is that a hickey on your neck? A asks.

Our unexamined appetite—

The myth of gender, animal, of what we are and can become.

Play me flamenco, show me the snapping!

Pretend we are driving and driving, my head out the window, the desert a drowning, the desert a cool bomb—

Bullrich Salt trickles out of a sack along the desert ground . . .

The old woman shoots Ringo, her dog.

Coyote wounds in a ring around his neck and rear end. Maggots got into him. She cries.

I remember when Ringo was born. He looked like a worm.

She buries him on the hillside.

A boy runs down the hill, ear flaps to his cap cocked in the wind.

A girl in a college classroom sniffles. Her six-thousand dollar purse has gotten dirty. Someone in the room says, *Sob story.*

I don't want to be alive to be negated, A said this morning.

All these negations. All these small jacks and no rubber ball. Marbles in a pot-hole, lost in dirt.

The man in gloves taps his foot, waiting for the holes in the earth to fill. Then he stuffs the hose back in its metal bed, clamps the faucet, and pours the leftover bucket of liquid down the last open hole.

How to withstand death?

If I just try hard enough to equally desire and not, can I will postcolonialism to exist without apocalypse?

See the cover of *Postcolonialism: A Historical Introduction.* I will dress the part of the French soldier or the Algerian woman . . .

But the answer to ending affliction is not changing sexes, races, places—

Look at Israel in Palestine.

John Brown was a hero, but have you ever seen his statue at the farm? His giant arm around a tiny slave?

I still have scars from sleeping alone. This can't be the only way.

Flammable 1203 on the side of the gloved man's truck.

A lot of dirty puddles and spring-blossoming trees by the side of the road.

I remember the rock of my father's fireplace. What good does memory serve?

Miniature porcelain pots crack underfoot.

Above them, I unroll a spool of red thread. Burrs stick to my long cuffs. Squat, white-tufted birds that look like B make off with my yarn—

Come back!

Mechanical Reproduction

The empty building that could have been
any other building, but was not.

One man crumbles in front of it, having returned
after so many years. *I lost so much,* he cries.

Gnats swarm around his head. A friend's arm
steadies him. They are here to confront

those who now dance
mechanically with ghosts—

Ein, zwei, drei.

The dancers remember their lines—
so ingrained, so memorized.

This one yells. That one moves repeatedly
across the bowed floor.

The roof, an arrow, points to what was done

to families, children. Blood was taken.
Eyes opened and closed.

Photographs, stacked like plaques,
have molded together. It's hard to separate

one face from the next.

One man's hand unburies a face
from the dust, his finger traces

the chin's dimple.

The tortured look into the camera.

It is an age in which men and women and children
are destroyed and remade in the machine's image.

A lone cricket, silent, on the balustrade—

A's B (a memory)

I have womanly hips, B says proudly, flaunting them as he walks into my kitchen in his occidental blue cloth wrap.

I want him in the pure way of want. Not as spirit or saint. His hair smells (wet and unwashed) of animal, unpleasant humanness.

He undresses just my lower half. I pose like the statue in the park by the lake, with one hand pointing up, the other down.

Our monument to each other is our proclaimed indifference. My hurt past, not to mention his impotence names us.

His spine ends, abruptly, unendurably dipping into a concave pool above his ass.

Unendurably, because this can't last. *What will we do,* he asks, *now that our bodies are meant for each other?*

He has me up against cool walls. Our androgynous selves merge and thighs bruise. We are the right heights.

We are no longer who we fantasized we could be—our spleens suspended, timeless. There is no escaping the future in which B will accuse me of Chinese courtesy and I will call him fascist.

The angel across the lake with furious wings frowns as B grabs me, finalizing what can't be made final.

The child, B will write in a letter I'll treasure—

The Specter

In the moor, prisoners with spades.

A child, elsewhere, sprinkles
mushroom spoors onto a page.

Benjamin stops digging the frozen ground
to scratch his face from a photo.

His friend tells him: *Your nothingness is
the only experience the age may have of you* …

You and your nothingness, my friend says.

We are in her car. She has asked me
what I want for my birthday.

Ghosts of material things—

like the child

(disappointed the spoors haven't yet bitten
the paper) with soft, decaying teeth

who sucks on a piece of winter
sugar on snow, maple
wings,

(having already spun
themselves silly) asleep for the winter
in his mother's red geranium pot.

After finishing his treat,
the child sighs,

full and glistening like a seed,
buried, waiting.

Another Childhood, 20th Century

The rug was brown. It lay in the living room in front of the arched, stone fireplace. My father, mother, and I would roll around on it until static stood our hair on end. Then we would shock each other. Little electric sparks in a house without electricity.

The coffee table was made from a cherry tree lightning split. The dining room table was walnut. Fashioned together in three pieces, it wasn't large. The surface was dark. The grain ran one way. Hot dishes would scar it, make the wood even darker.

I sat in my grandfather's highchair. It had a woven, wicker back and could be set at three different heights; collapsed, it was a buggy. One of its metal wheels was broken. The tray's wooden edge was loose. The whole chair wiggled.

My father's writing was kept in the old wooden ice-chest under the telephone. Even as a girl, I sensed his words held clues to a family narrative silenced by death. In the woods behind our house was a spring box. I was the water bearer, swinging empty gallon jugs across split-log bridges to get to where the clean water flowed—

The Progress of the Lamplighter

crepuscular, brittle exoskeletons,
not to be touched, firewing

monarchs, cabbage butterflies
milkweed, coffee cans

gauze tails dipped in kerosene,
wound up and down,

potato beetles, naked blue
in the middle, yellowing inside,

turning black and cancerous
in glass jars, superbright

the more lamplight I become
holding the fragile globe

the more soot is borne aloft
in the scared-of-the-dark night

Intersection of Appearance and Disappearance

O
He rings the bell; no one comes (495)

P
blind alleys (523) horses stumble (524) tread with bare feet only (525)

Q
spyglass (535)

R
whispering of gazes (542)

S
mirrors back darkly (545) "with the gaze of silk" (549) when they sought his body, they found nothing, / Only a flower with a yellow center (550) the empty over the full (351) the hollow form over the filled form (557)

T
electric light (562) during the night (563) "Smile of the Dead" (570) Glare (570)

From Benjamin's *The Arcades Project.*

First Generation (1929)

C writes with her left hand, squirreling away the paper, curving it toward her. B studies her handwriting. She studies his hands, the gestures he makes. She knows from his forefinger and thumb that he is self-conscious and strong-willed. She picks up on his homo-social self by the way he strokes his mustache. Looking at her writing, her script, B is sure of C's bisexuality. Nevertheless, he asks her to write in pencil. He pays attention to the arabesque of each letter. She looks like a boy. Her long nose pronounces her face. Her jaw is thin. B's been paralyzed by his love for a boy as smooth-skinned as she. This boy carried himself straight, and his handwriting looked like shell-streaked sand. This boy wrote with his whole body—the way little animals' carapaces are pressed into and dragged across the wet earth by pull of tide—unintentionally smudging each letter (when he wrote with his left) with the outer palm of his hand.

C senses from the way B waves, hand quivering, like a wind-riddled feather boa, he belongs to another century, another gender. He inhabits his body like a bicyclist rides a giant three-wheeler—perched on top, his movements up there tiny in comparison to what happens below which is made mysterious by his half-frightened, half-delighted, dissociated engagement.

B is married with a son. His wife mimics the son's script and uses the son's name to seduce her lovers. B is a knowing accomplice in his wife's search for the love of her life, and his wife, likewise, teases him about C.

B wanders the street at night. He thinks of pursuing C, but actually he is tired. There is simply nothing left in his heart—no other man to be. He's been three. Loved three women—each with a four-letter name. They've all left him. He no longer wears a red tie. He's also shared himself down to his glasses—the most intimate of possessions—with a boy who wrote with his left hand when he was a man, his right when he was a woman.

C knows when B invites her to dinner, by looking at his library, that he is not happy. He speaks about children—the way they gesture freely and thereby bring the dead, unwittingly, back to life. Children, C agrees, are what to think about when everyone says nothing can continue. Children who cruise through malls, looking left and right, then injecting themselves with hormones when they aren't doing anything else in bathrooms. They are the ones who see anew, changing the landscapes of their bodies to fit the arcadian rhythms of the city, their hands heart-breakingly nimble, almost impossible to categorize; their handwriting giant, colorful, decorative, and the ownership they take of their signatures at once ominous and enviable.

Second Generation (1978)

In *Germany in August,* F is naked,
his limp penis part of his pitiful aggression.

His friends have just been murdered
in their prison cells.

The government of old
Nazis claim

his friends killed themselves.

F films himself using state funds.
Watch me watch, he cries.

He tells the story quickly, urbanely,
yelling at his mother

who romanticizes
a *ganz nett* future leader.

Then he pounds his lover's back.
And when his lover leaves,

he pounds the doorframe.
Three times.

I know how the story ends.

Maybe this is why I want to crawl
into F's pocket,

be his cigarette consumed in flame

and exit—
a smoke ring, hanging

halo-like above an empty bedroom.

Another World

How the hidden little hunchback mocks B, halves his portions, his desire, squealing, then grabs B's binoculars and tries to weasel his hand into B's pocket, where time ticks at the end of a chain. Enslaved, B touches A's lips. He promises he'll improve. And she, sarcastic, sighs, *The hours of lovemaking?* To which he, sincere always, replies, *No, A, we'll talk more—I'll feel closer.* He is still standing, his hand touching A in the middle of the street—

Flashback to this: A lesbian scene in Proust, B's hand covering A's left eye. Moscow, the theater, B excusing himself, Proust's sadism fluffing a completely unexpected, beautiful breast. B's sobs.

The arcade, loggia, iron ring set in stone, cliff dropping to the sea—why did B turn around there, and face the flip book, shadow puppet, ice-rink, and leave the scurrying letters on the page to their grey selves?

Well, to begin with E gives B drugs, records B's trips, observes B's face as it changes in fullness, writing down what B says: *Remain identical a while longer!*

A snowy egret, neck twice the size of its body, could be B, collar buttoned, red tie tied to hide the lump he swallows, as A, waving, grows smaller.

B tells E about materialist magic—another way to circumvent, short-circuit the fascist attempt to make magic immaterial. As he speaks, his hand becomes E's hand. An enchanted laugh. Morphine amazes. B and E cross into the forest B described long ago. E sees the *legs of elephants sway like fir trees,* then the *hesitant little trees,* the *snappy trees,* and finally *two pine trees together seem to jump.* B and E—two stuck typewriter keys.

Let Go

knife clasped between teeth, breath held——wrestling from the depths the beloved *pearling*

a clasped shell against which B lays his head, listening to the phantom sea inside crash

floats, ever lighter, until, seemingly nose to nose with the lily

divests him of the country in which he has been living. He unclasps

As if a tiny man stepping out of a pomegranate or a bead of blood, open-winged, defenseless

orders a dozen oysters, rolling the pearl around

anticipated this emptiness. Laying there, heart open

Stuffed, unbuttoning the top of his trousers, B says it is always the same world, memory just a bath, agitated by whoever wishes to see what

pearl, between thumb and forefinger, shimmers

Benjamin's Spectacles

Dead Benjamin asks me for a cup of coffee. I shake my head. He is dressed in red tights. Feathers in his hat. The kind of dandy who cannot admit his desire. He'll focus on some point in conversation, so as not to betray his gaze, his intonation vague, and lose sight of what called the attention he craves. He dreams of flying backwards, his back to the illuminated horizon, haloed. Our marriage was fatal. *Nothing left except the dregs,* Benjamin says. I am now the cup's brim, the floral pattern, the heavy doll whose eyes creak open with false lashes. Wig fallen, my sticky, bald head not worthy of Benjamin's spectacles, not worthy of the smoldering watercolor of his eyes. He opens the black trunk. Inside, my porcelain arms and legs are splayed, my head flung back, eyes closed. Beneath me, in the dark, the grandfather clock's indelible, gold stamen. The coffee's cold. The spectacles glint, menacingly, beside the cup and saucer.

Beside the Cup and Saucer

I

One mouse
made of thistle,
lacquered, beheaded.
Its hands still hold
the make-believe
cheese.

II

I eat breakfast
in front of pictures
of the tortured.
I've taped their glare
to the wall.
Their blurred faces
void of expression.

III

Simone Weil believed
to have war in the body,
to know war intimately,
was to be blessed.
Like her, I have warred
my body. Yet I remain—
I look at myself
with contempt,
not only in the mirror,
but at the parts I can see:
I hate them.

IV

Plant, fireplace, window shade, beige couch.
Children's clasped hands. A boy's large feet. A girl's hyper smile.
The colonel erect. Wife all dolled up. Table, wine, banal conversation.

The Universal Gaze

The angel of the future talks about herself at a horribly high pitch.
Now she's slamming doors.
She is simply bored.
I empathize.
The war has lasted so long the sight of blindfolds is no
longer novel.
Everything is splattered, scattershot.
The angel of the future has no want to
pick up the pieces or awaken the dead.
Instead, she steals my spectacles and screeches,
Every eye from now on must be made uniformly!
My nickel rims are the last thing I see before
lasers scan me.
I wait interminably, it seems, for shadows.
Each speck of light burns.

Intersection of Agriculture and Genocide

U
emancipation of the flesh (591) with its "sacred smoke" (594)

V
conspiracy organized in the house of a charcoal dealer (616)

W
our storehouses, our wealth (625) musk roses, golden plums and fresh pineapples (632) wild boar (632) leveling of roads (635) barbed wire (638) a mesh—between herding, plowing, and gardening (648)

X
dead matter (654) the concealment of labor (670)

Y
moonlight asserts its rights (690) improvised grimaces (691)

Z
like lice (694) bloated with fat (694) evil to love and embrace (696) scattered along the banks of rivers (697)

From Benjamin's *The Arcades Project.*

Revolutionary Evidence

Isolated

in the soul breaker,
a revolutionary

(before being murdered
by his guards)

writes a letter,
asking his love

would she be willing to
do it in the road:

Look at these
spring ruts.

Contents of an Envelope Stamped 'Refused'

I keep thinking your name is ever,
ever after. I cannot place you
in a seaside grave. Like a wife
trying to recover, I cannot find
your body. I feel so betrayed,
so shaken by it all. I suffer.
And just as the medium obeys the voice
that takes possession of him from beyond
the grave, I stand up and throw sod
over my shoulder. Now I can't remember
my own name. I crouch back down
in the ditch, rehearsing for death,
allowing agriculture to approach,
my body plowed, ready to be sown.

On the Dying Author

People wrap trees with trash to shame them into bearing fruit,
and then, during war, they place faces there, and skin, hair, teeth.

Montage

Spring arrives
on genocide watch
and whistles far
and wee expectantly.

The wind blows.
But no butterfly
comes—just the goat-
footed balloon man
over snow-capped
mountains, clapping
his hollow bell.

Listen to him huff!
Word-like clouds
hover around him.
His little hooves
stitch the snow
in cable knit
hoofprints.

It's spring.
The little man
shivers.

A Brisk Spring Wind

May fled to a place so barren
  as to be of no contest.
                  Like the parents
                    of the child
In white dunes, she had the nerve
    to become male.
    Really, she was bloodless,
                  on her lap
                    in this photo,
      a woman with hair
        around her breasts.
                  dead-too-soon,
     She wore a vest.
                  April existed
     Her brothers shut their eyes,
                  in harms way
      though they tried to have her exiled.
                  to pay the living
                  for the dead.
     May almost did disappear when,
        in the midst of being caressed
          by the loving words of a telegram,
        she heard a crack.
                  Under-eating
      She collapsed.
         Had her skull been split?
         (convinced she could carry
          Looking up, she saw a saber.
         a girl's body),
            Why? she wailed.
             she blew away.

My mother stands by the window puffing her sacred smoke.
Inside, my father conspires and throws another log on the fire.
Sugarplums in a bowl by the pineapple's rough husks. Outside,
the howl of a coyote. Javelinas rummage through garbage,
snorting, strewing compost. My mother curses, chasing them
through the streets in the darkness. My father and I play
a final game. He moves a dowel. Through the window, the moon
stares. I am not adept at the psychological way he plays, pretending
angst. *Don't look at me like that,* I cry. Invisibility my only defense.
He doesn't want me to go. It's my turn. I stay (even though
he thinks I am moving) with one of those moves that do nothing.
My mother comes in, stomping snow from her boots.
Where's Spring? she asks. I wrap my hands around hers, a muffler
she removes, unknowingly. She and my father embrace by the fire,
lonely shadows against stone walls, trilobite spines, fossil-spirals.

Communiqué

For Immediate Release

We, post-angels of a burgeoning era, met today to discuss progress in implementing a method to make Spring hide from what's in front of her.

We welcomed the progress: Her hollow eyes, decayed mouth.

We therefore underscored the importance of preparing ourselves for what will happen when interrogations are over, masks removed.

We reviewed pledges made last year that must be delivered in a predictable manner, for if not, what will be left?

We also looked forward to hearing about the desert fire, noted the substantial progress made of nuclear proportion, and welcomed the decision to allow the sunset.

We noted a camel, a stone.

We urged donors to contemplate what it will mean, after this free-for-all theft of it all, to hate, to want to destroy, to own.

We called on seventy dead again today to prepare for a more challenging environment, and noted the interest covered in cardboard on the street.

What to do with the bodies: We welcomed the implementation of hands tied and asked for a subsequent progress report.

We stressed the instances of dead bodies, like Benjamin's, either missing, or like this one [see accompanying image], lying face down.

We also celebrated how something may be eaten from the inside and still appear, although more needs to be done to welcome the seer grafted to this occurrence from afar.

We recognized the importance of the horrifying thing.

And we wish to thank everyone who does not suffer at all.

Underground

Wearing umbrella leaves—
Ticks, pine needles, ants—
Time passes me by—
Squeeze my leg—
Concrete in my hair—
A rock glows white—
Measure the snow—
Grab your penknife—
Tell me again how to get up—
Put my hands by my sides—
Lift my knees—
Nick my height—
I reach to your swallow—

The Disembodied Voice

I drive up to the old woman's house with the one center window in the middle of the burned field, past the fence stuffed with Styrofoam cups that spell *LOVE U ORESTA*. The old woman tells me about her feeble legs and skeleton face, and her friend (married now, with children) who punched her in her sand-blown skeleton face—all because of one bean and one leaf. They were fleeing war. One bean and one leaf was all they had to eat; they had to share, and her friend—a man-skeleton—didn't want to. She's in her pea patch. She stops talking and points under her house. *Blossom had puppies!* she whoops, slapping her thigh. Her voice is unselfconscious. I've heard it other places. I've heard it at the Exxon. The old timer who calls me Spring Chicken has the same voice. It goes up and up. It soars. A funny falsetto filled with lots of laughing and giggling and then boom, it breaks. Then it rises again. True to the hills. The old woman wears a shirt with dogs on it. I look at where she recently burned herself. Her fleshy hand—not so skeletony now—is pink under the burn. *It's a different sound, sung in a different tone of voice,* she says. *Soft as a voice of an angel,* she sings. At first the melody is recognizable, but then she shifts to a high-pitched, drawn-out, fluttering moan. The high, untranslatable, unnotatable voice, the fairy voice, the voice eternally a ghost child's long lost shadow, floats at the same time as it is held down. This voice comes from clothes under gowns, from submersion in polluted rivers carrying no-contact advisory warnings. I pray without praying to the old woman. She's down now at the riverbank, hugging her knees, cursing her own reflection in the flaccid scum of the polluted tributary. The light bouncing off the rippled river casts a white line across her neck, slicing her in two like quartz cuts through a dark stone. I remember my skeleton face and the selfishness of it when I think about her abandoned skeleton. I imagine the people we used to be and who we are now, this spring, as she dips her bucket into the water, hauls it uphill, and shows me how to grow.

Transparency

A skeleton confronts me:
Whose body are you trying to make matter?

I say:
I respond to knives with food.

The skeleton clucks:
Keep your hands clean.

intersection of cartography and telling time

d
nothing beautiful but what is forgotten (753)

i
disoriented survivors (786)

k
female corpses (790) heaped-up paving stones (795)

l
marsh farmers brought their vegetables to town (799)

m
Empathy (805) how depressed one had to be (806)

p
The dead are "multiform" and exist in many places on the earth at the same time (816)

From Benjamin's *The Arcades Project.*

lament of light

i

what was the collapse? when did it occur?

there were orange peels on a wood cook stove, drying. i put them in my pockets before going to school. i liked their aroma. sometimes i nibbled on them. the wood cook stove stood cock-eyed to the kitchen; you passed it on your left as you headed toward the window. i remember standing near it and wishing i wouldn't have to eat. i was twelve.. already i had been told i would have to go to the doctor if i didn't straighten my shoulders.

how did you unbury yourself?

it was spring—i could not let myself roost, curled, feverish with approaching light as doves huddled on fence posts. the morning shower chilled. i wanted to be able to reconstruct my body before i allowed the light in—light choked by suffering birdsong. instead, i stretched past the limit of my own skin, limiting touch, trading the arc of what is not, for the flavor of what was.

shivering woman whose skin comes upon you like that of an infant, who can claim you?

the fist that never rested.

ii

i decorate the refrigerator. *why do you put things on it?* the refugee asks. he has never had a refrigerator. i am not asking for anything. i don't open my mouth. there are a billion unmentionables.

the task isn't something that can be assigned, it is a becoming—a becoming linked to a gesture, a fossil imprint. regret, take back your silver hair from my shoulders. don't require me. we favor the mirror, we favor the refrigerator.

you cannot awake unknowing. water travels down. we are fed by circumstantial rain, seasonally. mesquite blossoms coat the sand. i brace myself for the emergence of sun. it is beyond the horizon, blocked by what's in front of me. soon it will be blocked by what is behind.

totem pole

i turn on the radio, dust on it.
it is playing a bolero. my hat is round
and brown, the color of broken dirt.
the night again is cold. i do not sense
spring or change. car doors slam.
i carve a dowel with my pen-knife
into a stick figure. in its eye-sockets
i glue silver dollars. they shimmer.
out of place in the metropolis, hands
gripping my hat, i hawk my doll.
involuntary memory, i call it, because
already i miss what i must give up.

walter benjamin at the mechanic's shop

the End of History is the lost stage. take this mechanic's shop for instance, where i sit, absorbed in benjamin, while men poke around on trucks. at the End this shop must be empty, the metallic shells of vehicles its only remains. everyone here, even the pot-bellied manager, a ghost.

the End is not being able to see. i do not mean the lost gaze of a person in terror or a person who has lived through the promise of nothing, but rather not being able to see (not from the inside, but from the out) what is in front of you—like this shop.

i may, for example, not be reading benjamin well. likewise, the men at this shop may tinker all day, start engines, and not repair a particular mechanical problem; the work we do invisible to one another like the beggars we drive past whose desperation reminds us of the connectedness of our separateness and, hence, our foreclosed feeling. we say we do not have a dollar.

i read and the men work on trucks—each of us doing nothing more than meeting to exchange labor. i do not pay attention to the trucks being serviced. the mechanics, similarly, ignore me reading in the over-heated foyer. there is no place in this shop for there to be an event.

last night, at a luxurious table of food with champagne, talk of the world without humans, how it will survive. this End of History—in which no one will be left to record what happens—is, perhaps, the result of disappearances that increasingly take place without protest. it is, too, the barbarism of my reading while others beg.

what confounds those who write History is the inability to be able to kill everything, including galaxies. the End of History, therefore, is species dependent and simultaneously the End of something that has never taken place or existed for more than half the people on this planet. in other words, anyone who is dying may very likely have been someone who was never alive, at least for the purposes of those present and past chroniclers of History.

and so, i sit here on this lonely stage, wishing to turn back, for it is clear now that i am no revolutionary volcano, just a lowly actress reading her part—my white truck (up in the air on a hydraulic lift) purely a stand-in for mother courage's groaning, good-for-nothing, wooden cart.

history with a little h

the man who thinks kindness
a weakness related to women, says

(we are in bed and
i have asked him a question):

i forgot women talk.

he is used to sleeping
with men. he assures me

he will hurt me. i tell him
i am hurt already.

the room is dark.

you haven't dealt with your past,
he says. *how can i?* i cry.

a miniature plastic bull
stands in half-prance
on the shelf.

i know better than not to bet
on who'll gore whom.

when i was walter benjamin,
a woman helped drag me

up a mountain.
could that woman be this man?

i bow my head and let him stick the darts in.

notes

page 21   *Behold me, what I suffer because I have upheld that which is high*
           —Edith Hamilton

page 27   *I don't throw bombs, I make films—Rainer Werner Fassbinder*

page 27   *Each man kills the thing he loves—Oscar Wilde*

page 28   *I will fight you like a woman... You in those towers, I will be back*
           —Jennifer Harbury

page 28   *America is a friend ...—a sign outside Abu Ghraib prison, Iraq*

page 52   *Remain identical a while longer; legs of elephants sway like trees; hesitant little
trees; snappy trees; two pine trees together seem to jump—Walter Benjamin*

page 45   *...do it in the road—George Jackson*

page 46   *And just as the medium obeys the voice that takes possession of him from
beyond the grave—Walter Benjamin*

acknowledgments

Benjamin's Spectacles could not have been forged without support from my east Kentucky and Tucson friends and mentors; you all have strengthened my writer's heart. A special thank you to Al and Robin Ulmer, poet Sonia Sanchez, and Lisa Bowden of Kore Press—without you, this publication wouldn't exist.

author

Spring Ulmer holds a B.F.A. from The Cooper Union School of Art and an M.F.A. in Poetry from the University of Arizona. Her honors include grants from the Kentucky Arts Council, the Kentucky Foundation for Women, and the Andrea Frank Foundation. She lives in Iowa City.

colophon

Benjamin's Spectacles is set in Eric Gill's lean, forthright and humanist typeface Gill Sans. The running text is Light and display weight is Regular. Pages were designed and typeset on a Mac PowerBook G-4 using InDesign during the month of May and corrected during June. Book work took place in the new Kore offices on Country Club and in my new home in Poet's Corner, at the intersection of Whitman and Longfellow. While the author and her mother put 2000 strawberry plants in the ground in upstate New York, Eve and I put layers of mud onto the walls of my healing room in the house, and this manuscript was made a book.

The cover illustration: Spring Ulmer sent me the clouds—which I colorized and manipulated—and the spectacles, which she painted. Twenty years ago in a park in Paris I took a photograph of the statue which appears in one of the lenses.

The Chinese character seen on the title page is purported to be the symbol for poetry, though recent searches have not yet revealed that translation. Over some years it has made its way from the desk of Debra Gregerman, artist and writer, onto many of our broadsides—stamped from a hand-carved, soapstone chop—then to our website, our letterhead, and now, into our books.

press

As a community of literary activists devoted to bringing forth a diversity of voices through works that meet the highest artistic standards, Kore Press publishes women's writing that deepens awareness and advances progressive social change.

We have been celebrating the genius of women through publishing since 1993. Greek for *daughter* and another name for Persephone—the goddess whose re-emergence from the underworld marks the changing of seasons—the name *Kore* expresses our belief in the power of the creative process and our conviction that women can change the world.

To see our publications and programs, to support the work of the Press, or for information on submitting a manuscript, please contact us at www.korepress.org.

Kore Press artists

Renée Angle
Jennifer Barber
T Begley
Lucinda Bliss
Eavan Boland
Camille Bonzani
Olga Broumas
Vicki Brown
Wendy Burk
Becky Byrkit
Barbara Cully
Alison Deming
Ann Dernier
Ani DiFranco
Deb Esarey
Karen Falkenstrom
Deborah Fries

Maggie Golsten
Mary Gordon
Jorie Graham
Debra Gregerman
Anne Guthrie
Niki Herd
Jane Hirshfield
Linda Hogan
Marie Howe
Dolores Kendrick
Elline Lipkin
Sandra Lim
Tedi López Mills
Audre Lorde
Nancy Mairs
Nancy Mendoza
Cynthia Miller

Jane Miller
Shelagh Mulvaney
Martha Ostheimer
Marge Piercy
Adrienne Rich
Desirée A. Rios
Frances Sjoberg
Elizabeth Cady Stanton
T.C. Tolbert
Brenda Ueland
Spring Ulmer
Sylvia Um
Joni Wallace
Faith Wilding
Tiphanie Yanique
Ofelia Zepeda
Sarah Zimmerman

Kore Press acknowledges

Arizona
Commission
on the Arts

NATIONAL
ENDOWMENT
FOR THE ARTS

why publish women?

1. In the history of the National Book Awards, only 29 percent of the winners have been women.

2. In early 2005, women constituted only 17% of the opinion writers at *The New York Times*, 10% at *The Washington Post*, 28% at *US News & World Report*, and 13% at both *Newsweek* and *Time*.

3. Of the 137 authors in the most recent *Norton Anthology of American Literature*, less than one-third are women.

4. The official poster for 2006 National Poetry Month, sponsored by the American Academy of Poets, includes 18 quotes by famous poets. Only 25 percent of those poets were women.